D1592198

SCHIRMER'S LIBRARY
OF MUSICAL CLASSICS

Vol. 1992

ALEXANDER SCRIABIN

Piano Sonatas

ISBN 0-7935-3011-3

G. SCHIRMER, Inc.

Distributed by

Hal Leonard Publishing Corporation

7777 West Bluemound Road P.O. Box 13819 Milwaukee, WI 53213

CONTENTS

SONATA NO. 1

I

Alexander Scriabin, Op. 6
(1893)

5

6

12

a) Possible:

a) Alternate:

II

molto rit.

III

Presto ♩. = 132

a) Possible:

IV

Funereal ♩ = 50

a) Possible: b) Possible: c) Possible:

SONATA NO. 2
Sonata-Fantasia

I

Alexander Scriabin , Op. 19
(1892-97)

34

a) Possible: b) Possible:

II

Presto ♩ = 96 - 100

p sotto voce

cresc.

mf

dim.

p

45

SONATA NO. 3

I

Alexander Scriabin, Op. 23
(1892-97)

51

II

a) Possibly:　　b) Possibly:

a) Likely:

57

III

58

IV

a)

N.B. In the fourth movement the barely feasible passage in the Presto, with its basic figure

was played by Scriabin himself with the following alteration, allowing him to take a fantastically quick tempo:

62

a)Possible:

SONATA NO. 4

I

Alexander Scriabin, Op. 30
(1903)

73

attacca

II

Prestissimo volando ♩. = 160

Holding back

SONATA NO. 5

I summon you to life, hidden aspirations!
You, buried in the dark depths
Of the creative spirit, you, timid
Embryos of life, to you I bring daring.
(*The Poem of Ecstasy*, p. 11)

Alexander Scriabin, Op. 53
(1907)

Allegro; wildly capricious

Presto; joyfully

Allegro fantastico
molto accel.

Presto; tumultuous, exalted

Allegro impetuoso

accel.

Leggerissimo volando   accel.

Presto giocoso

a) Possibly:

a) Strictly speaking, this note may be omitted (Scriabin's annotation).

SONATA NO. 6

Alexander Scriabin, Op. 62
(1911–12)

fleet; like a whirlwind

sudden terror

poco più vivo

sotto voce

mys- terious call

more and more carried away, with enchantment

charmed

poco cresc.

a)

mf

m.d.

a) Alternate:

piùvivo
with joyous exaltation

118

all becomes charm and sweetness

fleet; like a whirlwind

123

sudden terror pervades the dancing delirium

In the right-hand chord, the note d of the fifth octave, which did not yet exist on the keyboard was changed by Scriabin himself to c, i.e.

a)

SONATA NO. 7
"WHITE MASS"

Alexander Scriabin, Op. 64
(1911–12)

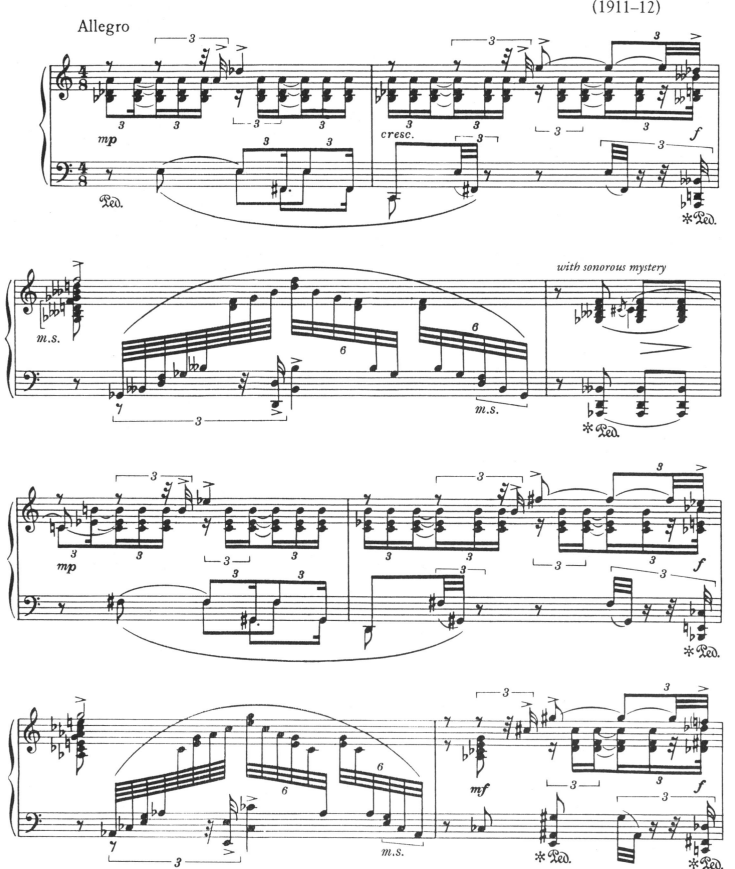

128

132

Tempo I

thunderous

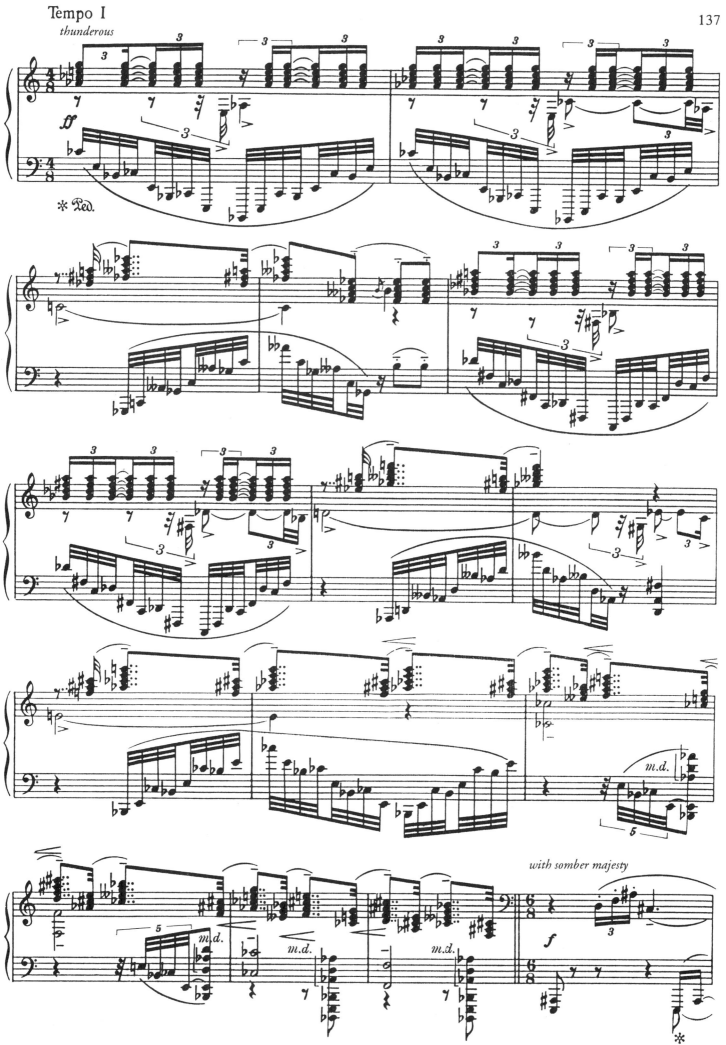

accel.

SONATA NO. 8

Alexander Scriabin, Op. 66
(1912–13)

Allegro agitato

a) Likely:

Tragic

Tragique; Molto più vivo

Allegro (Tempo I)

a) Possible:

175

gentle, languishing

a) Alternate:

SONATA NO. 9
"BLACK MASS"

Alexander Scriabin, Op. 68
(1912–13)

Moderato quasi andante
as if recounting a legend

molto accel.

Molto meno vivo

pure, limpid

Allegro

accel. poco a poco

Allegro

SONATA NO. 10

Alexander Scriabin, Op. 70
(1912–13)

Allegro

Powerful, radiant

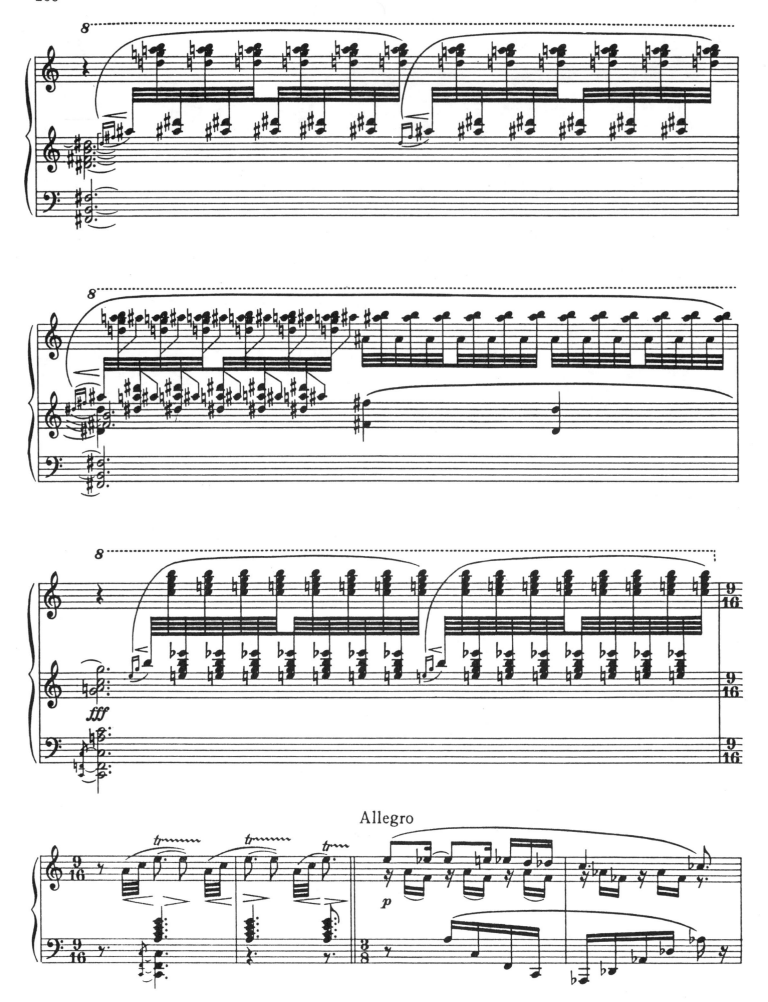

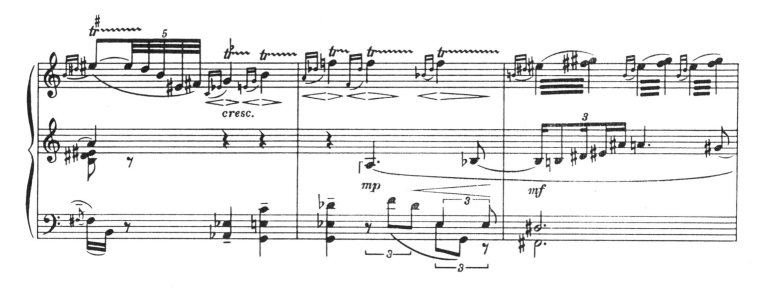

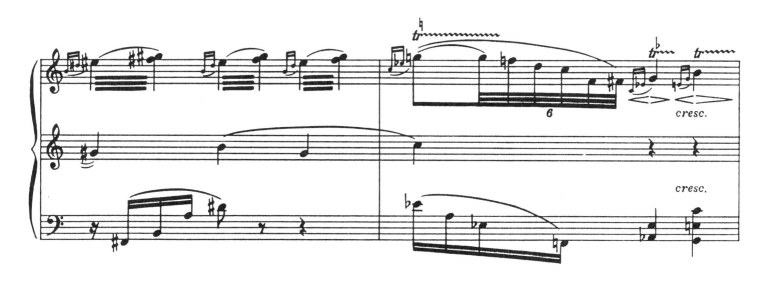

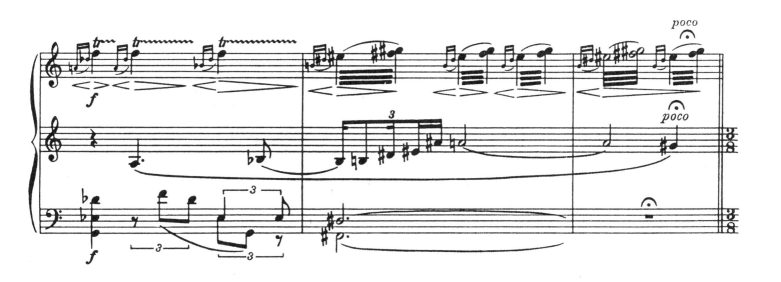

212

Moderato *with gentle, fading languor*